FOCUS ON MIDDLE SCHOOL

Biology

Laboratory Workbook

Rebecca W. Keller, PhD

Cover design: David Keller
Opening page: David Keller, Rebecca W. Keller, PhD
Illustrations: Rebecca W. Keller, PhD

Focus On Middle School Biology Laboratory Workbook
ISBN 978-1-936114-54-2

Published by Gravitas Publications, Inc.
www.gravitaspublications.com

Printed in the United States

Keeping a Laboratory Notebook

A laboratory notebook is essential for the experimental scientist. In this type of notebook, the results of all the experiments are kept together along with comments and any additional information that is gathered. For this curriculum, you should use this workbook as your laboratory notebook and record your experimental observations and conclusions directly on its pages, just as a real scientist would.

The experimental section for each chapter is pre-written. The exact format of a notebook may vary among scientists, but all experiments written in a laboratory notebook have certain essential parts. For each experiment, a descriptive but short *Title* is written at the top of the page along with the *Date* the experiment is performed. Below the title, an *Objective* and a *Hypothesis* are written. The objective is a short statement that tells something about why you are doing the experiment, and the hypothesis is the predicted outcome. Next, a *Materials List* is written. The materials should be gathered before the experiment is started.

Following the *Materials List* is the *Experiment*. The sequence of steps and all the details for performing the experiment are written beforehand. Any changes made during the experiment should be written down. Include all information that might be of some importance. For example, if you are to measure 237 ml (1 cup) of water for an experiment, but you actually measured 296 ml (1 1/4 cup), this should be recorded. It is hard sometimes to predict the way in which even small variations in an experiment will affect the outcome, and it is easier to track a problem if all of the information is recorded.

The next section is the *Results* section. Here you will record your experimental observations. It is extremely important that you be honest about what is observed. For example, if the experimental instructions say that a solution will turn yellow, but your solution turned blue, you must record blue. You may have done the experiment incorrectly, or you might have discovered a new and interesting result, but either way, it is very important that your observations be honestly recorded.

Finally, the *Conclusions* should be written. Here you will explain what the observations may mean. You should try to write only *valid* conclusions. It is important to learn to think about what the data actually show and what cannot be concluded from the experiment.

Laboratory Safety

Most of these experiments use household items. Extra care should be taken while working with all chemicals in this series of experiments. The following are some general laboratory precautions that should be applied to the home laboratory:

Never put things in your mouth without explicit instructions to do so. This means that food items should not be eaten unless tasting or eating is part of the experiment.

Use safety glasses while working with glass objects or strong chemicals such as bleach.

Wash hands before and after handling chemicals.

Use adult supervision while working with sharp objects and while conducting any step requiring a stove.

Contents

Experiment 1: Putting Things in Order   Date: _____

Objective   In this experiment we will organize a variety of objects into categories.

Materials

Collect a variety of objects. Some suggestions are: rubber ball, cotton ball, orange, banana, apple, paper, sticks, leaves, rocks, grass, Legos or building blocks, etc.

Experiment

❶ Spread all of the objects out on a table. Carefully look at each object and note some of its characteristics. For example, some objects may be smooth, some fuzzy; some may be edible, others not; some may be large, some small, etc.

❷ Record your observations for each item in the *Results* section.

❸ Now try to define "categories" for the objects. For example, some objects may be "hard," so one category could be called "Hard." Some objects may be "round," so another category could be "Round." Try to think of at least 4 or 5 different categories for your objects. Write the categories along the top of the graph in the *Results* section.

❹ List the objects in the category that describes them. Take note of those objects that fit into more than one category. Write these objects down more than once, placing them in all of the categories that describe them.

❺ Next, take a look at each of the categories and each of the objects in those categories. Can you make "subcategories?" For example, some objects may all be the same color, so "Red" could be a subcategory. Some may be food items so "Food" could be a subcategory. Pick three categories and try to list several subcategories for each of these main categories.

❻ List the objects according to their category and subcategory.

Results

Item	Characteristics

Categories						

	Categories					
Categories						
Sub-categories						

Conclusions

_____
_____
_____
_____
_____
_____
_____
_____
_____
_____
_____
_____
_____
_____
_____

Review

What is taxonomy? _____

_____

List the three domains.

_____   _____   _____

List the six kingdoms.

_____   _____

_____   _____

_____   _____

List the other six categories for classifying living things.

_____   _____

_____   _____

_____   _____

Which kingdom are dogs, cats, and frogs in? _____

Which phylum are dogs, cats, and frogs in? _____

Which class are frogs in? _____

Which order are dogs in? _____

Which family are cats in? _____

What is the Latin name given to humans and what does it mean?

_____

_____

Experiment 2: Inside the Cell   Date: _____

Objective   Using the drawings of the three types of cells in the student text, we will observe which features of the three different types of cells are similar and which are different.

Materials

 pen or pencil
 colored pencils or crayons

Experiment

Write down some things you observe in the drawings that are similar for all three cell types: _____

_____

_____

Write down some observations of things that are different: _____

_____

_____

Write down the function of each of the following:

  nucleus _____

  mitochondria _____

  chloroplasts _____

  cell wall _____

  lysosome _____

  peroxisome _____

How do animal cells differ from plant cells, and how do both plant and animal cells differ from bacterial cells?

List as many differences as you can between bacteria, plants, and animals, and explain why you think their cells may differ.

Archaea/Bacteria (have or don't have...)	Plants (have or don't have...)	Animals (have or don't have...)

Without looking at your textbook, fill in the blanks with as many names for the structures in the cell as you can. Color the cell.

Is this an animal cell, a plant cell, or a prokaryotic cell? Write the cell type at the top.

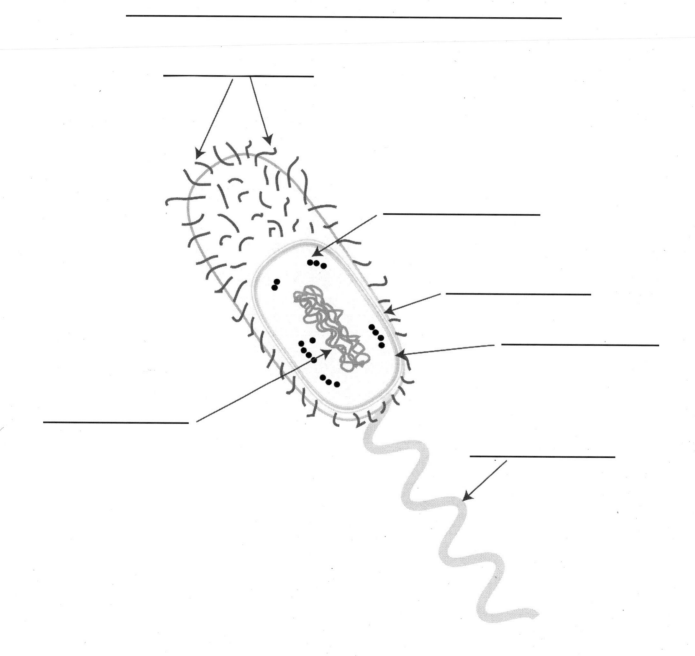

Without looking at your textbook, fill in the blanks with as many names for the structures in the cell as you can. Color the cell.

Is this an animal cell, a plant cell, or a prokaryotic cell? Write the cell type at the top.

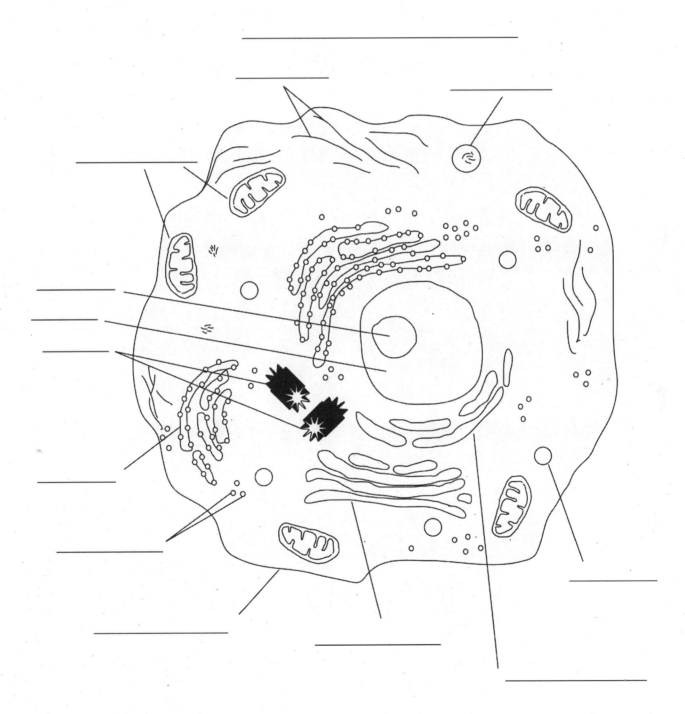

Without looking at your textbook, fill in the blanks with as many names for the structures in the cell as you can. Color the cell.

Is this an animal cell, a plant cell, or a prokaryotic cell? Write the cell type at the top.

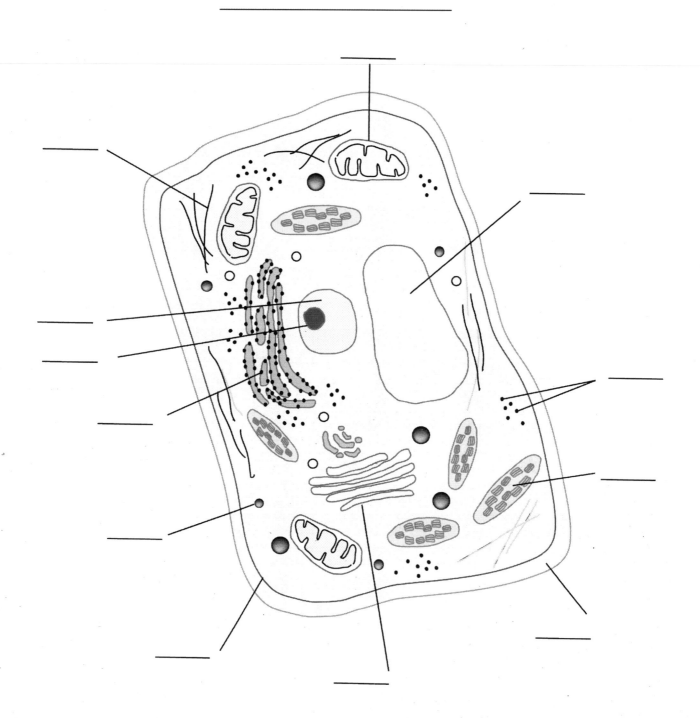

Conclusions

_____

_____

_____

_____

_____

_____

_____

_____

_____

_____

_____

_____

_____

_____

_____

Review

Answer the following questions:

What are cells made of? _____

_____

What are tissues made of? _____

_____

What are organs made of? _____

_____

Define the following terms:

prokaryote _____

_____

eukaryote _____

_____

organelle _____

_____

Name some organelles found in plant and animal cells:

_____   _____

_____   _____

_____   _____

What does a flagellum do? _____

_____

Where are chloroplasts mostly found? _____

_____

What are mitochondria for? _____

_____

Experiment 3: Take Away the Light   Date: _____

Objective   _____

_____

_____

_____

_____

Hypothesis   _____

_____

_____

_____

_____

Materials

> plant with at least 6 flat, green leaves
> lightweight cardboard or construction paper
> scissors
> tape
> 2 small jars
> marking pen

Experiment

❶ Take some cardboard or construction paper and cut it into squares large enough to completely cover a leaf. Make enough pieces to cover the front and back of 3 leaves.

❷ Six different leaves will be tested. Two of the leaves will be left on the plant (attached) and four leaves will be removed from the plant (unattached).

❸ Using the cut out cardboard pieces from Step 1, tape two pieces so they cover the front and back of one of the two attached leaves. The other leaf will stay uncovered. Remove four leaves from the plant. These unattached leaves will be either covered and placed in water, uncovered in water, uncovered out of water, or covered out of water.

❹ With the marking pen, label the leaves in the following manner:

Leaf 1:   UA — uncovered, attached

Leaf 2:   CA — covered, attached

Leaf 3:   UUW — uncovered, unattached, in water

Leaf 4:   CUW — covered, unattached, in water

Leaf 5:   UU — uncovered, unattached (no water)

Leaf 6:   CU — covered, unattached (no water)

❺ Take two small jars and fill them with water. Take the two leaves that will be placed in water and prop one in each jar, keeping the stems submerged. Check the water level every day over the course of the experiment to make sure there is enough water in the jars.

❻ Wait several days, and then every day observe the changes to the leaves. Carefully remove the cardboard from the covered leaves to make your observation, and then re-tape it. Record your observations.

Results

	UA	CA	UUW	CUW	UU	CU
Day 1						
Day 2						
Day 3						
Day 4						
Day 5						
Day 6						
Day 7						
Day 8						
Day 9						
Day 10						

Conclusions

_____

_____

_____

_____

_____

_____

_____

_____

_____

_____

_____

_____

_____

_____

Review

Define the following terms:

photosynthesis _____

_____

chloroplast _____

_____

chlorophyll _____

_____

conifer _____

_____

algae _____

_____

cyanobacteria _____

_____

How do most green plants get their food? Do they eat cheeseburgers?

_____

_____

_____

Experiment 4: Colorful Flowers   Date: _____

Objective   _____

_____

Hypothesis   _____

_____

Materials

2 or more small jars
2 or more fresh white carnation flowers
food coloring
knife

Experiment

❶   Take two or more of the small jars, and add water and several drops of food coloring to each.

❷   Trim the end of one carnation stem, and place it in one of the jars of colored water.

❸   Watch the petals of the carnation, and record any color changes observed.

❹   Take the carnation out of the jar, and cut a small slice of the stem off the bottom. Try to identify the xylem and the phloem. In the *Results* section, draw a picture of what you see. Cut the carnation flower lengthwise. Try to identify the parts of the flower.

❺   Take one stem and slice it lengthwise with a knife, starting about halfway up the stem and cutting away from the flower. (Have an adult help you.) Stick one end of the divided stem into a solution of colored water, and place the other part of the stem in a jar that contains water of a different color. Let the carnation soak up the colored water until the petals begin to change color. In the Results section, draw a picture of what you observe.

Results

Color change in carnation placed in one color water

Color change in split carnation placed in two colors of water

Conclusions

_____

_____

_____

_____

_____

_____

_____

_____

_____

_____

_____

_____

_____

_____

_____

Review

Define the following terms:

xylem _____

_____

phloem _____

_____

pith _____

_____

pollen _____

_____

stamen _____

_____

ovary _____

_____

Name the four main parts of a flowering plant:

_____   _____

_____   _____

Name two types of roots:

_____

_____

Experiment 5: Which Way Is Down?   Date: _____

Objective   _____

_____

Hypothesis   _____

_____

Materials

2 small jars
several dried beans (pinto, navy, etc.)
absorbent white paper
plastic wrap
clear tape
2 rubber bands
knife

Experiment

❶   Cut strips of white paper to fit around the inside of the jars.

❷   Label each strip with the letters "A", "B", "C", and "D" leaving a few centimeters between each letter.

A	B	C	D

❸ Place the beans so they face in different directions on the labels, and fasten them with clear tape. They should look like this:

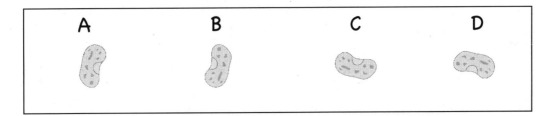

❹ Place the paper with the attached beans gently inside the small jar. The beans should be between the jar and the paper.

❺ Place one or two more beans in between the paper and the jar, but don't tape these. These beans will be opened and examined before the roots completely emerge.

❻ Add some water to the bottom of the jar, but don't submerge the beans.

❼ Cover the jar with plastic wrap and secure it with a rubber band. Place the jar in direct sunlight.

❽ Using the second jar, repeat steps 1-7, but place the jar in a dark place like a closet.

❾ In a few days the beans will start to grow. When the beans begin to change, take out one of the loose beans and gently cut it open. Try to identify the different parts of the embryo.

❿ Continue to observe the growth of the beans. Watch and record their changes every few days. Try to determine if the beans placed in different directions grow differently, and compare the beans grown in the light with those grown in the dark.

Results

Draw the parts of the embryo in the box below.

Record your observations for each bean. It may be several days before you see a change. Record the number of the day that you observe a change, and draw a picture of the way each bean looks on that day.

DAY _____   **LIGHT**

A	B	C	D

DAY _____   **LIGHT**

A	B	C	D

DAY _____   **LIGHT**

A	B	C	D

DAY _____   **LIGHT**

A	B	C	D

DAY _____   **DARK**

A	B	C	D

DAY _____   **DARK**

A	B	C	D

DAY _____   **DARK**

A	B	C	D

DAY _____   **DARK**

A	B	C	D

Conclusions

Review

Define the following terms:

seed _____

_____

seedling _____

_____

seed coat _____

_____

cotyledon _____

_____

embryo _____

_____

germination _____

_____

Name two plant signals.

_____

_____

List the four stages in the life cycle of a flowering plant.

_____

_____

_____

_____

Experiment 6: How Do They Move?   Date: _____

Objective   _____

_____

Hypothesis   _____

_____

Materials

microscope with a 10X objective
microscope slides
3 eye droppers
fresh pond water or water mixed with soil
protozoa study kit
methyl cellulose

Experiment

❶ Familiarize yourself with your microscope before beginning this experiment. Read the instruction manual for your microscope, if it is available, and try to look at any prepared samples that may have come with your microscope. If you already know how to operate a microscope, skip this step.

❷ Take one of the samples from the protozoa kit, and place a small droplet onto a glass slide that has been correctly positioned in the microscope.

❸ Observe the movement of the protozoa. If the organisms move too quickly, apply a droplet of methyl cellulose to the glass slide.

❹ Patiently observe the movement of one type of protozoan. Note the type of protozoan you are observing in the *Results* section. Try to describe how the protozoan moves. Draw the protozoan, and write down as many observations about its movement as you can.

❺ Repeat Steps 2-4 with the other two protozoan types.

Results

Name of protozoan _____

Describe movement:

Name of protozoan _____

Describe movement:

Name of protozoan _____

Describe movement:

❻ Now take a droplet of fresh pond water (or water mixed with soil) and place it in the microscope. Try to determine the types of protozoa you are observing based on how the organisms move. Write and draw your observations in the *Results* section.

Results

Draw what you observe in the pond water.

Conclusions

_____

_____

_____

_____

_____

_____

_____

_____

_____

_____

_____

_____

_____

_____

Review

Define the following terms:

protist _____

_____

cilia _____

_____

flagellum _____

_____

pseudopod _____

_____

Draw a paramecium.	Draw a euglena.	Draw an amoeba.

How do euglena and paramecia move? _____

_____

How does an amoeba move? _____

_____

Experiment 7: How Do They Eat?   Date: _____

Objective   _____

_____

Hypothesis   _____

_____

Materials

> microscope with a 10X objective
> microscope slides
> 3 eye droppers, measuring cup and measuring spoons
> protozoa study kit from Experiment 6
> baker's yeast
> distilled water
> Eosin Y stain

Experiment

❶ Color the yeast with Eosin Y stain:

- Add 5 milliliters (one teaspoon) of dried yeast to 120 milliliters (1/2 cup) of distilled water. Allow it to dissolve.

- Add one droplet of Eosin Y stain to one droplet of yeast mixture. Look at the mixture under the microscope. You should be able to see individual yeast cells that are stained red.

❷ Get the amoeba sample, and place a small droplet of the solution onto a glass slide that has been correctly positioned in the microscope.

❸ Take a small droplet of the yeast stained with Eosin Y, and place it into the droplet of protozoa solution that is on the slide.

❹ Looking through the microscope, patiently observe the protozoa, and note the red-colored yeast. Try to describe how the protozoa eat. Write down as many observations as you can. Draw one of the protozoa eating.

❹ Repeat steps 2-4 using the paramecium sample.

Results

Observations of an amoeba eating:

_____

_____

_____

_____

_____

_____

Draw a picture showing how an amoeba eats.

Observations of a paramecium eating:

_____

_____

_____

_____

_____

_____

Draw a picture showing how a paramecium eats.

Conclusions

_____

_____

_____

_____

_____

_____

_____

_____

_____

_____

_____

_____

_____

_____

Review

Define the following terms:

stigma _____

_____

food vacuole _____

_____

phagocyte _____

_____

oral groove _____

_____

cytoplasm _____

_____

What is a Didinium? _____

_____

_____

What is a Podophrya? _____

_____

_____

Experiment 8: From Caterpillar to Butterfly Date: _____

Objective

_____

_____

Materials

locally collected caterpillar and food, or butterfly kit
small cage

Experiment

❶ Place your local caterpillar in a small cage and provide food for it, or follow the directions on the butterfly kit for proper care of your caterpillar.

❷ Fill out the life cycle chart on the next page.

❸ Over the course of the next several weeks, observe any changes your caterpillar undergoes.

❹ Record how much food your caterpillar eats.

❺ Record how many times the caterpillar molts.

❻ Record where the caterpillar spins its chrysalis.

❼ If you are able to observe the caterpillar emerging as a butterfly, record how long it takes before it can fly.

Draw the various stages in the life cycle of a butterfly.

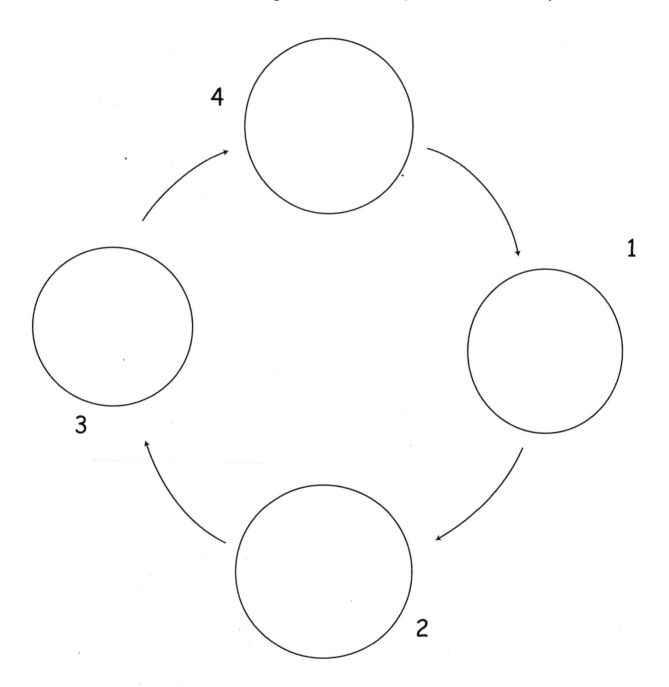

Results

Week	Amount of Food Eaten	Molting?	Other Observations
1			
2			
3			
4			
5			
6			
7			
8			
9			
10			
11			
12			

Conclusions

_____

_____

_____

_____

_____

_____

_____

_____

_____

_____

_____

_____

_____

_____

_____

Review

Define the following terms:

Lepidoptera _____

_____

larval stage _____

_____

molting _____

_____

pupal stage _____

_____

chrysalis _____

_____

imago _____

_____

Experiment 9: From Tadpole to Frog   Date: _____

Objective

_____

_____

Materials

tadpoles collected locally (or tadpole kit)
tadpole food
small aquarium
tap water conditioner and tap water (or distilled water)

Experiment

❶   "Cure" the tap water by adding tap water conditioner. This removes any chemicals, like chlorine, that would be harmful to the tadpoles and frogs.

❷   Fill the aquarium 1/2 to 3/4 full with the conditioned water.

❸   Add the live tadpoles.

❹   Look on the internet or in the library for directions for feeding your tadpoles. If using a tadpole kit, feed the tadpole according to the directions.

❺   Observe the changes the tadpole makes over the course of 4 to 6 weeks.

❻   Record your observations in the *Results* section. See if you can identify the different stages of the tadpole that are outlined in this chapter of the student textbook. (Note when the legs emerge, note the time it takes for the front legs to emerge, etc.)

Draw the various stages in the life cycle of a frog.

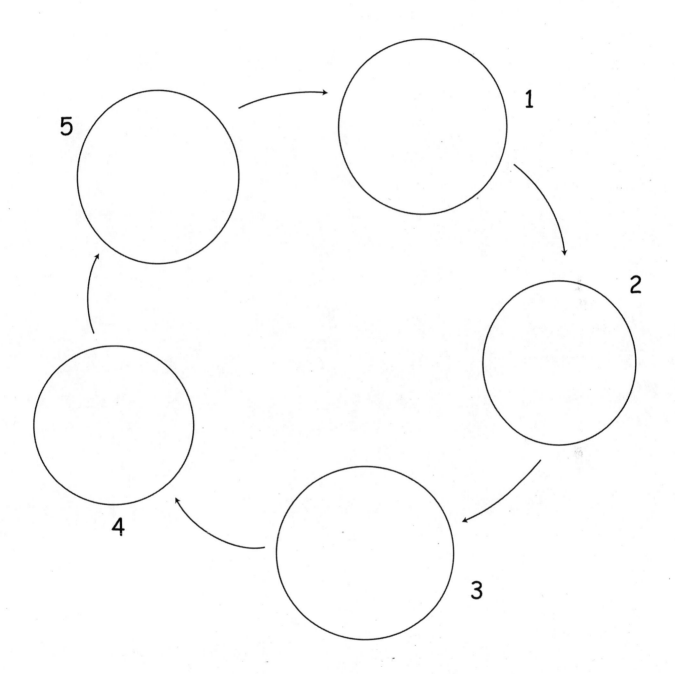

Label the parts of the frog.

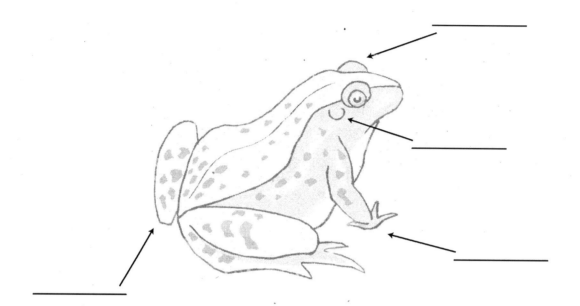

Results

Week

1 _____

_____

2 _____

_____

3 _____

_____

4 _____

_____

5 _____

_____

6 _____

_____

7 _____

_____

8 _____

_____

9 _____

_____

10 _____

_____

11 _____

_____

12 _____

_____

Conclusions

_____

_____

_____

_____

_____

_____

_____

_____

_____

_____

_____

_____

_____

_____

Review

Define the following terms:

spawning _____

_____

amphibian _____

_____

metamorphosis _____

_____

tympanic membrane _____

_____

Experiment 10: Making an Ecosystem —— Date: _____

Objective

_____

_____

Materials

clear glass or plastic tank with a solid lid
water
plastic wrap
soil
small plants
small bugs such as worms, small beetles, ants, etc.

Experiment

❶   Take the glass or plastic tank, and cover the bottom with water.

❷   Cover the tank securely with plastic wrap, and allow it to sit overnight.

❸   Record your observations in *Part I A* of the *Results* section.

❹   Remove the plastic wrap and let it sit overnight again.

❺   Record your observations in *Part I B* of the *Results* section.

❻   Place the soil on the bottom of the container. Put in enough soil to fill the container about 1/3 full. Add some water if needed.

❼   Plant the small plants in the soil.

❽   Add the small bugs to the tank.

❾   Place the lid on the tank. This is now a small closed ecosystem.

❿   In *Part II* of the *Results* section, record any changes in your ecosystem that occur over the next several weeks.

Results

Part I

A _____

_____

B _____

_____

Part II

Week # _____	Week # _____	Week # _____
Week # _____	Week # _____	Week # _____

Conclusions

_____

_____

_____

_____

_____

_____

_____

_____

_____

_____

_____

_____

_____

_____

Review

Define the following terms:

ecosystem _____

_____

_____

cycle _____

_____

_____

food cycle _____

_____

_____

air cycle _____

_____

_____

water cycle _____

_____

_____